fragments
of
dreams

a book of poems by
C.J. QUASAR

Published in the United States by The Wiggly Tree.
www.thewigglytree.com

Copyright © 2017 Claire Jacques.
All rights reserved.

ISBN: 0692629165
ISBN-13: 978-0692629161

for Bear

Acknowledgements

As I write this, I am asking myself, does anyone ever actually read the acknowledgements section in a book? Except the people who are being acknowledged, of course. But then I have to answer, I'm sure there are at least a few people who do, because *I* read acknowledgements pages. So, in honor of people who read acknowledgements pages, and, of course, the people being acknowledged, here is my gratitude to the people to whom I owe a greater debt than I could ever repay, even if I were a coffee-fueled workaholic who never slept and who made a superstar's salary.

Shoutouts go out first to ***my mom and dad***, who have stood by me for so long and with such immense fortitude that it can't possibly be expressed in words. They have encouraged my creative endeavors at every turn, and I love them dearly. Also to ***my brothers and sisters: Meredith, Roger, Megan, Peter, Lisa, and Max*** for expressing interest in my work and helping me make it happen. And to everyone else in my family who has helped me fight the inner critic by being so supportive. Best. Family. Ever. Seriously.

To ***all the teachers I've had over the years*** who told me they thought my work was awesome. That means a lot to me and keeps me writing. And the teachers I had in college who taught me graphic design – it's because of them that I was able to do the layout for *Fragments of Dreams*. Especially that teacher I had years ago whose name I wish I could remember. He taught me how to use the QuarkXPress publishing and design software, which enabled me to figure out Adobe InDesign, which is very similar and which I used to design this book.

4

To *Colleen Haley*, a teacher I had years ago who absolutely loved my writing and once gave me an A+++++ for something I'd written. I wish I'd kept it, but I still have the memory!

To *all the great people who write online tutorials* about InDesign and proofreading and the other stuff I needed to look up when making this book. They put that information on the internet for free, out of the goodness of their hearts. Their advice and expertise was invaluable in putting this book together.

To *Scott Krems,* who is my #1 fan, and whose tireless cheerleading has kept me working on other things while I was laying out this book, so there will be lots more books after this one, and other neat things too. Thanks, Scott. You rawk. :3

To *the leaders and writers of the IC Saturday Morning Writers' Circle*, for their friendship and enthusiastic support. You guys rock. Especially *Mary Kistner*, who is also my #1 fan and a tremendous inspiration.

To *Gwyn Morford Pearson and Christy Frank Liming,* for encouraging me to get my work out there for people to enjoy and for inspiring me with their own creative stuff. They're also my #1 fans. I've known them since about 1997 (which, incidentally, was approximately when the first of these poems were written) and they've been infallible friends since.

And to *everyone else who loves my stuff*, of whom there are far too many to list and still have a book of poems, not an encyclopedia of acknowledgements. You're all my #1 fans, and much appreciated!

Table of Contents

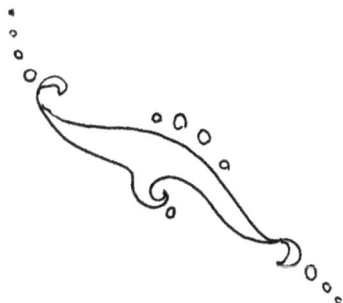

Colors of Shadows

nightning is what I call it
when the whole world is dark
it strikes down at ground zero
like a black and shadowed spark

I wander in the darkness
until I've reached the end
and at that point, I give new names
to the shadows I befriend

there's ebony and onyx
there's cockroach black, and then
there is the color of the pupils
of the eyes of twenty men

there's blackdog, and there's inky black
the opposite of white
and then there is the space between
the stars that shine at night

nature abhors a vacuum
so these colors never last
but you can sometimes see them
if you look into the past

Love Song of the Spanish Inquisition

I love you with the might and main
that sinks the greatest ships;
I love you with the mortal pain
that parts the tightest lips;
I love you with the desperate force
that marks a dying hour;
all love is torture and remorse –
it shall my soul devour.

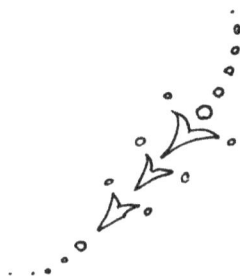

Angels in the Architecture

Shadow box against the wall
frescoes painted in the hall
gargoyles on flying beams
and angels on the roof.

Panthers growl from every cloud
I see them, but I'm not proud
I know not from whence they came
the angels on the roof.

Wrought iron fence, a great oak tree
wooden door under lock and key
greenery cut like animals
and angels on the roof.

Vaulted ceilings, stained glass tales
steep staircases with year-smoothed rails
ancient musty air within
and angels on the roof.

I can't speak to the masonry
so I know not its history
and I surely cannot ask
the angels on the roof.

A shattered glass ceiling
the lead paint on the walls is peeling
climbing roses cannot reach
the angels on the roof.

Candlelit in every room
dust settles in the gloom
I look up, and only see
the angels on the roof.

Rusted weapons in the armory
a dark basement of anarchy
gardens untended for generations
and angels on the roof.

Vegetable gardens grey with blight
shattered glass bulb that sheds no light
mirrors on the ceiling
and angels on the roof.

The next room of the dream
unicorn hair upholstery seam
sunlight wafts through broken windows
and angels on the roof.

An ancestor accessible restroom sign
the place I sleep that is not mine
scrubbing a demon off the kitchen floor
and angels on the roof.

Fnords in every other floorboard
an icebox with a dragon's hoard
a china cabinet with the Holy Grail
and angels on the roof.

An outhouse of stone and light
casements pulled shut against the night
dying flowers in flowerbeds
and angels on the roof.

In the parlor, a clavichord
every ploughshare turned to sword
spiral staircase into nowhere
and angels on the roof.

Kitchen stocked with nothing I need
a library with books I cannot read
a morning glory by my window
and angels on the roof.

Rusted nails hold the thing together
from years of neglect and stormy weather
marble sculpture on the grounds
and angels on the roof.

The Land of I Don't Know

I have been to the land of I Don't Know.
I don't know how to get there
I can't tell where to go
looking at the map, I don't have a prayer
'cause I don't know what it's supposed to show

when I'm there I don't know my name
or what my itinerary's got in store
I can't even remember why I came
I don't know anything anymore
I don't know why everything's not the same

I asked the people here the questions I had
I don't know how to tell you they didn't know too
I can't tell if I feel good or bad
I'm not sure if anything's false or true
I don't know if that was ever anything that I had

I don't know the language that they speak
but neither does anyone else
and I don't know why I feel like such a freak
I try to remember but nothing is ringing bells
It's amazing I even know how to speak.

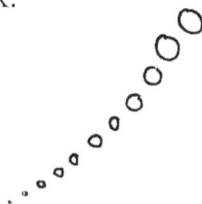

Candle

Shining light
lovely against the night
glowing so soft and bright
until the hint of the sun

candlelight
reaching an orange height
hypnotic to my sight
when each of my days is done

the voice of the One

gentle mind
speaking to me in kind
and they say love is blind
but only in the dark

what will I find
after the smoke has twined
and my face has grown lined
and my life has grown stark

lit only by a spark

Lines Scrawled on a Sticky Note Found in a Wastebasket at the Copywriting Department of a Major Greeting Card Company

I wrote you a beautiful little note;
you would hardly believe it was something I wrote.
But I dropped it somewhere along the way,
and now I'm stuck with nothing to say.

I wrote you a totally spiffy love letter;
Shakespeare himself couldn't have done it better.
But I lost it somewhere – I swear it's true!
So I guess this one will have to do.

Observations

On a cold morning in January
a boy is weakening;
he fights away death,
dreaming of kittens
and chocolate milk.

On a hazy day in November
two lovers are fighting;
a crystal vase hits the floor,
leaving twinkling shards
all over the upholstery.

On a moonlit Tuesday
a woman is shopping;
she walks the aisles,
looking for pureed beets
in the aisle marked "borscht."

Who Knows?

What would happen if a little Suppose
cunningly clad in a Maybe's clothes
inched up, and crept up, and tipped on its toes
and sat down at the end of one of the rows
of stiff-necked and straitlaced Yes's and No's?

I Want to Be

I don't want to be lonely.
I don't want to be alone.
I want to be like the guy
with the snazzy tie,
the one in the commercial
for the expensive cologne.

Yeah, that one.

Weird Dream

I had the weirdest dream last night.
It really freaked me out.
The strange things I saw happening
could never come about.

I saw a guy with a shirt on
woven all of parrot hair.
And everyone was equal,
and all were treated fair.

I saw a dog with sixteen feet
that were black with golden flecks,
and there was no pornography,
and no one lived for sex.

I stared at tiger-striped planes that flew
over fields of talking wheat.
And everyone had a place to stay
and something good to eat.

And when I woke up from that zany dream
I scolded my psyche (to wit:
none of that stuff could ever happen!)
Ludicrous, isn't it?

Finally

For the past year I've been keeping score:
scars on one side, jewels in my crown
on the other.
And finally
in the twilight of the year,
they've come out even.
And none too soon.

Balance

Follow the spiritual, as you may;
walk the straight and narrow way.
But play in the dirt, too, and eat onion rings,
for part of life is the earthly things.
Strike a balance between the two;
your true heart will tell you what to do.
You can't get there with spirit alone,
so play outside 'til it's time to go home.

I Remember Him

He liked jazz. That
is what I remember. Mumbling scat
to himself
in time to the beat
of the tapping of our feet
on the pavement
was the way he would say what he needed to say

He wasn't as smart as me.
That is what I remember. But
he loved hard, called me baby girl,
knew who I was
without my needing, even, to tell him at all.
My fancy words always fell useless to the ground
before even I could say them.

One night
I was sad
so he made me write
in a notebook for a while
'til I cracked a smile

One summer we rode our bicycles
on a gravel trail.
I remember.
They say they made it out of an old railroad,
tearing up the track
until only the little rocks were left
to bite at our skinny road tires.

We haven't ridden since,
but the trail is still there, lying
on the earth: a lazy sidewinder.
Sometimes it makes me think of him,
the man with the saxophone
who liked jazz.

I wonder if he remembers.

Runner's Prayer
For my dad

God, grant me extra energy
to get up off my buns,
for it almost sounds like scripture:
good things come to him who runs.

Sometimes I just don't want to leave:
it's too hot, too cold, too wet.
But all the times I've come to you for help,
I've made it out there yet.

I'll look to You for guidance
when my muscles start to ache;
when I just can't make it further,
this humble prayer to You I'll take.

When I start to suffer,
help me take it like Your Son would do
and help me get back safely
when I bite off more than I can chew.

Send Your angels out to follow
and protect me from the rain and snow,
for I know they won't get tired
however far I go.

And while I'm at it, thanks
for all the good my running does;
each new day that begins,
I'm so much stronger and faster than I was.

I thank you also for the way
my muscles stretch and strengthen.
I know I've got you on my side
when my runs begin to lengthen.

Thank you, Lord, for all the wonders
Your creation can provide;
it's all because of You
that some days I ever get outside.

The handiwork of man provides
sidewalks and rubber track,
but it's You I thank for the cooling wind
and the warm sun on my back.

So, as I head forth from the warmth
of my beckoning bed,
as sure as wearing running shoes,
this prayer will be inside my head.

For though sometimes it's difficult
to get up out the door,
you've come through in the past, Lord,
and I'll keep coming back for more.

Instructions for Being Human

Fly without wings
weep without tears
own without things
age without years

Run without ground
sing without words
scream without sound
sky without birds.

"Build a better mousetrap and the world will beat a path to your door."
~ Ralph Waldo Emerson

* * *

Cheese Whiz

There once was a guy from North Pass
who improved the design of mousetraps.
Sure enough, when we'd seen
his spring-loaded machine,
we hiked to his doorstep *en masse.*

Garbage Flower

Darkness around
ships run aground
and I flourish
dancing in the endless night
coal-bright
I grow
trash around me
deranged mind found me
I bloom
oil-slick ocean
hard world in motion
I live
cut off from the dark
standing stark
I watch
scabbing over hard
dark gods' ward
I cry
protected by my pain
forever I've lain
I am
a garbage flower

it's some kind of power

"Quod me nutrit me destruit."
(That which nourishes me, destroys me.)
~ Christopher Marlowe

* * *

Pills

I have white ones to keep me stable
brown ones for the pain
pink ones to sedate me
and yellow for the visions in my brain.

There's blue ones for the anguish
red ones for the fright
and purple ones to help me sleep
'cause I woke up three times in the night.

I have orange ones for the headaches
green ones for the stress
and I have twelve others to take as needed
for the side effects of all the rest.

Well, the other day I spilled them all
though I opened the bottles with care
and after a moment's deliberation
I decided to just leave them there.

Musings on the Nature of Escargot

There once was a guy from North Wales
who developed a taste for fried snails.
While eating his lunch,
he would say mid-munch,
"Delicious – and good for what ails!"

Inscription on a Tree Trunk

Enter thou this Leafy Haven
If you are willing to Eschew
The truth that you are Thirty-Seven
And the things that grown Men do

If you can Forsake your Prudence
Perch upon a mighty Bough
Take shelter in this green Domain
And forget the Here and Now

Guardian

We walk alone together
one in kind, two brains alike as only genii can be
separated from the world, earth not.
Extending feeble tendrils,
we find only one another.
I can live with that.
If I must make my way against the world
I'll need you.

Pretty creature,
what are you made of?
Mysterious.
You were not my first, but still that magic word
nous
resounds: sacred temple echoes.

You see?
Punning, our banter
mindless,
and still far above the world's conversation,
forges new links with every word wired.

Oh man of mine,
O crazy quilt, pieced of miscellany,
which of those have I have wanted to be?
You and I are cut of this same uncertain cloth
maybe
at once pale and dark,
nourished by the light of machines.

You
are my desert springs
and shiny things,
my crown, my pain, the fire in my eyes.
My heartstrings stretch awfully
with strides' distance.
To me you are beautiful
like barbed wire and starless nights are beautiful.

Perhaps I knew you
even before they cut off your wings,
but I've forgotten.
I will try to heal your wounds
anyway
you're worth the effort.
I glow when you call me
Guardian.
Let me stay by your side
and we'll walk,
forever together.
(Alone)

Hot

You shouldn't base your self-esteem
on another person's thought
but it helps me to remember
my boyfriend thinks I'm hot.

I know true beauty comes from within
but when I forgot
I ask my boyfriend what he thinks
and he says he thinks I'm hot.

Like all women, I am convinced that I am fat
even if people say I'm not
and the only thing I'll listen to is
that my boyfriend thinks I'm hot.

So if I think that I look bad
in the new clothes I just bought
I'll ask my boyfriend what he thinks
'cause he'll tell me he thinks I'm hot.

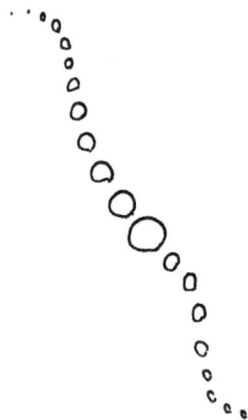

Why They Don't Put Bad Reviews on Book Covers

It languishes in dusty repose –
the paperback that no one chose.
Sits desolately on the shelf,
seeming sad all by itself.
But it really isn't hard
to see why someone would this book discard.

"Like an unfinished game of chess,
the ending hangs," the cover says.
"The rest is drivel, pond scum, trash –
it certainly isn't worth the cash.
If you'd a book this summer read,
choose another and pay this one no heed."

And so on in likewise manner,
on the cover like a repellent banner.
"Don't buy me," it seems to say.
"Choose another book today.
The worst book I've read in all my life!"
Shredded under the critic's knife.

No wonder no one wants to buy it.
They are all afraid to try it.
The critics have scared them all away;
they read another new book today.
And everyone who stops by and looks
sees why only good reviews are put on the covers of books.

"Love hath great store of sweetness, and 'tis well;
A moment's heaven pays back an age of hell."
~ R. W. Dixon

* * *

A Place to Claim Sanctuary

Sometimes it's brutal how hard an hour alone is.
That's when I long for my post-modern youth;
he's a kind of anti-classical Adonis,
his flesh dark marble, hard but fragile truth.

I come to him as day gives way to night,
resting by his side. His features, smooth with sleep,
are half-caressed by incandescent light
and perfectly at home in dark that deep.

O Mage, keep me alive with lyric breathing;
just rest. Don't ask what kind of fire burns
underneath this skin so hotly seething.
I dread the moment when the fear returns.

Dark angel, your rest douses your own ember.
Perhaps that's why you try to sleep all day.
Your heart is ripped alike when you remember...
O, draw me near, I'll kiss the pain away.

To hold and be held: such is modern magic,
an alchemy of touch, our mutual drug.
Remind me how my life is hardly tragic
as I foil your inner Hades with a hug.

Me and the Professor

Abstract art, he says,
hides an inability to draw.
Free verse, I think,
discloses an inability
to write.
All this as the models disrobe,
concealing nothing
but their own apathy.

Dire

toeing the line
sparks down my spine
casting about for recognition
but I know no one in this place
picking at my best scars
can't lose them
we drape our material bodies
for various reasons
and still can't get
where we are going
saying something beautiful with your eyes
I can't remember
how my lines
were supposed to go

*"Never offend people with style
when you can offend them with substance."*
~ Sam Brown

* * *

Obscenity Is for C***-S***ers

Once I read the d*** graffiti
some f***er scribbled on the wall,
while I tried to take a s***
in a g****** bathroom stall.

F*** that! What if it could offend
some poor f*** out there?
No one f***ing needs to read
that d*** c*** everywhere.

So it's my new g****** mission
each time I f***ing see
obscene s*** in print or on the air –
I'll make that b**** rated G.

What If

If God were a cat
He would prowl around the house on silent paws,
stopping every now and then to trap
some unseen evil
in His jaws.

And God could be a cat,
for it seems as though a cat is always there,
keeping nightly vigil by the hearth
or from beneath
every chair.

Yes, God would be a cat
if God could bend all creatures to His will
with no more than a knowing glance,
then gaze ahead,
gentle still.

Maybe God is a cat.
When I watch my kitten pounce upon a string,
I see my life beneath her claws:
a small diversion.
Everything.

If God is a cat
(and the nature of Divinity is doubt),
He is a fierce and lonely hunter
and the Devil
is a mouse.

Little Gun

asked politely for my hand
I said no way no how
you cut off something of mine you die
and I locked the question away
they say speak softly and carry a stick
but I prefer a gun
it's not a big gun but it works
it's mostly scary in fearful situations
I keep it loaded as a matter of course
I don't understand precisely how it works
but I know how to use it
you aim
pull the trigger
now not everyone has such good aim
but I do
from years of practice under duress
they say you can learn better that way
it's totally true
I hit the mark every time
no matter how formidable the foe
now who can say that of a stick
not I surely
you walk into a place of business with one of these
they are unlikely to stop you
as they are small and unobtrusive
I didn't ask for a little gun
I would have preferred something huge
an AK-47 perhaps
something that could do a lot of damage
they say this little thing can hurt
I didn't believe them
but then I've never turned it
on myself

Art

My friend.
My guardian.
My dark chocolate.
My home.
My secret lover at midnight.
My crown of thorns.
My release. My song.
My pleasure.
My heart. My soul.
My security blanket.
My rose-colored glasses.
My mask. My mirror.
My window to the world.
My love.
My imagination.
My job. My passion.
My curse. My life. My pride.
My secret.
My words.
My spirit. My religion. My truth.
My shelter. My hiding place.
My insanity.
My treasure map.
My learning curve.
My beauty. My future. My skill.
My savior.
My education.
My confidante.
My fascination. My nature. My words.
My road map. My song.
My heart of hearts. My lifeblood.
My iron curtain.
My secret code.

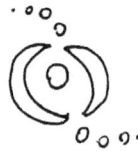

My barbed wire.
My humanity.
My locked door. My sacred ritual.
My inexplicable affinity. My inexorable desire.
My glass of single-malt whiskey hidden in the bottom drawer.
My band-aid.
My magic.
My warmth.
My world.

Things That Are Useless in Winter

Jeeps
motorcycles
convertibles
shorts
bikinis
ankle bracelets
toe rings
flip flops
sunscreen
pool toys
citronella yard torches
BBQ grills

so you either have to get rid of all this stuff
or move to Bermuda

The Pedestrian

I used to walk when the light said walk.
I waited patiently
until the rules said I could proceed.
But that didn't work for me.
Because one day I nearly got killed while crossing
by a driver heading home from the bars.
It's tough to be a pedestrian
in a world of cars.

So now I just try to wait until
the avenue seems clear,
and pray to the gods of the asphalt roads
that no one's been drinking beer.
But sometimes I'm wrong, and a driver will turn,
looking at me like I'm from Mars.
It's tough to be a pedestrian
in a world of cars.

Their headlights narrowed like angry eyes,
cars all seem out to get me.
One of these days I'll miscalculate
and one of them will hit me.
If one were just to tap me,
I'd be seeing stars.
It's tough to be a pedestrian
in a world of cars.

So if you're looking for me,
I'll probably be found
getting across a busy street
by taking the long way around.
Because crossing the road at the intersection
hasn't gotten me very far.
It's tough to be a pedestrian
in a world of cars.

Alone

When you're alone
you don't have to fake it
you don't have to try too hard
you don't have to smile
if you don't wanna
but maybe you don't
have any reason to smile
when you're alone

Insomnia

The door is closed.
The lights are off.
But I am still awake.

It may seem as if
I'm sleeping, but
the snoring's merely fake.

For there are poems
inside my head
that want to come out and play.

I wish that they
had said that when
it was still the day.

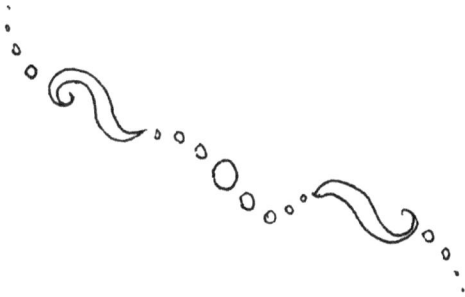

"I expect to pass through this world but once. Any good therefore that I can do, or any kindness that I can show to any fellow creature, let me do it now. Let me not defer or neglect it, for I shall not pass this way again."
~ Stephen Grellet

"A word is dead
When it is said,
Some say.
I say it just
Begins to live
That day."
~ Emily Dickinson

* * *

Unsaid

"A word is dead when it is said, some say."
Emily Dickinson wrote this in her day.
But there are no words quite as dead
as the kind things left unsaid.

Afraid of being thought a nerd,
you don't say you liked the music you heard.
But you would make your daughter's day
if you said you like to hear her play.

Too shy, you do not tell your sister
you're sorry she moved, how much you've missed her.
But words like these would mean so much
and keep two people from losing touch.

"I liked your play; you were really great!"
You don't say to a friend upon the stage.
But these words, if said, could be
a clarion call for a dying age.

We swallow our kind words every day.
Too busy, too scared, we had a bad day.
But if you say good things to a friend,
it will always turn out well in the end.

So don't hold back words of good intent.
Trust me, they'll know what you meant.
For there are no words quite as dead
as the kind things left unsaid.

"The victim said in a police report that he was checking out in the express lane when Mr. Golladay started counting his items. The suspect got irritated and told Mr. Golladay he had too many items to be in the '20 items or less' lane."
~ Jessica Chasmar, *The Washington Times.com*

* * *

Walmart Express Lane Haiku

Situation:
he tried to sneak 22
items through; got rammed

Birthday Song
to S.D., with love

On the anniversary of your birth,
I sing a happy song for you:
when the youthful smile that lights your eyes
meets the wisdom of your years,
and the universe that fills your mind
leads you to take what paths you will,
each day is like being born again.
May each passing day be joyous still,
and may you in your travels find
more reasons for laughter than for tears;
may friends light your way like fireflies,
and may every day bring as many gifts to you
as this day of merriment and mirth.

Notoctober

Who are you?
You are not
October.
Though you bear
the trappings
of Autumn:
a skyful of precipitous leaves,
denuded trees scratching
a washed-out sky with bony fingers,
a lazy sun with an early bedtime –
you are warm and mild.
A stranger.
The October I know
has an icy disposition,
most disagreeable.
And so
I do not know
who you are,
but you are not
October.

Beware

I saw a nightmare on the stair.
It didn't see me standing there.
And so I crept away with care
and managed to avoid its glare,
though I was left with quite a scare.
It chilled my blood and raised my hair.
And I thought, as I got away from there,
it could have caught me in its snare.
It could have dragged me by the hair
and hauled me away down to its lair.
It could have tied me to a chair,
and made me swear
at a grizzly bear.
If it had, I wouldn't have a prayer.
But it didn't – Fate chose my life to spare.
And so I'll tell you, if you take the stair,
just watch yourself, and take care
in case you see the same nightmare.

"Pork. The other white meat." ~ advertisement

* * *

It's What's for Dinner

There once was a guy from New York
who harbored a dislike for pork.
He never would eat
"the other white meat,"
so he only put beef on his fork.

Ace in the Hole

when Jerry was mad at me I remembered
    Mom still loves me
when my mom cursed at me I remembered
    Sal gives good hugs
when Sal slammed the door on me I remembered
    the cashier at Walmart smiles at me often
when the cashier at Walmart dropped my grapes I remembered
    my cat purrs at me
when the cat clawed me I remembered
    Kan brings me breakfast in bed on Mother's Day
when Kan crashed my car I remembered
    Lizzy likes my stuff on Facebook
when Lizzy made fun of me I remembered
    Jerry buys my paintings

... and I was never sad at all

Dying of Fear

I've heard of people dying of sadness
of laughter
and of pain
but I've never heard of anyone
dying of fear
I think I almost did
until I scared people so much
they saved me
it was strange
I clawed at the lid of my coffin
until my heart nearly stopped
and my father
who is connected to me by a connection fierce
and beautiful
reached down and picked me up
they carried me to the hospital
even though I wasn't sick, just resurrected
I'm afraid

Fall Hard

I came to my mother when I was still small.
I said, "They say love is the best thing of all.
But Joey is a huge jerk, and we got into a fight,
and he broke it off by email just last night."
My mother told me, "Honey, just let him go.
Love is the greatest thing you will know."
She said, "When you love again, forget that you're scarred.
And when you fall, fall hard."

In the ninth grade I went to summer camp by a lake.
But I was sure it was all a big mistake
when we did something the counselors called the trust fall.
I was scared and didn't want to do it at all.
So they called up my mother and she talked to me.
She said, "When you're falling you'll feel so free.
Just forget your fears and let down your guard.
Baby, when you fall, fall hard."

When my mother was eighty, she fractured her hip.
Her bones were weak and she fell from a slip.
The pain drugs made her not right in the head.
She told me, "I wish that I were dead."
Sometimes when one says that, she actually dies.
And my mother said to me as she closed her eyes,
"You don't want to die drugged in an osteo ward.
Sweetie, when you fall, fall hard."

At my mother's funeral it was snowy and cold.
My father looked bent, gray and old.
He tossed a rose on the coffin as they lowered it down.
Mom had died broken to pieces in a hospital gown
and that was the last memory Dad had of his wife,
who'd been a sultry spitfire every day of her life.
He said, "I have no regrets. She was worth it in every regard.
My darling, remember, when you fall ... fall hard."

The Party

While we were complaining about the coldest winter yet,
some historical figures were having a fête.

Columbus cooked turkey while Mao brought fried rice,
and everyone thought Dickens's sweetbreads were nice.

Paul Revere came on horseback while Gandhi just walked.
Caesar rode on a litter, and dead Kennedys flocked

to Olympus in Greece, but only because
Zeus' palace was where the party was.

Archimedes read theorems to Emily Brontë
while Napoleon swapped fruitcake recipes with Dante.

And no one brought gifts for the gift exchange
except Mussolini, which was kind of strange.

Marie Antoinette danced a minuet.
Even Einstein thought it was the best party yet.

Rosa Parks got drunk and sat on Tolstoy's lap
when Jesus made wine run from the tap.

But the party didn't get really rowdy
'til Pecos Bill showed up and no one said howdy.

Well, they danced and sang carols and drank Bach's eggnog brew
and partied and reveled 'til half past two.

For that, friends, is when the dreamer awoke.
(It was all just my brain's idea of a joke.)

Sylvan Gold

I saw a tree the other day; it made me think of you.
Its stolid branches seemed to say, "It is hard to stand here as I do."
How many more will have to weep before the spell is broken?
Who else will cry himself to sleep before the truth is spoken?

Experience warns of painful thorns that grow on blushing roses,
but no one will stay back until they feel the sting that touching poses.
And yet, the rose's pretty face continues still to beckon.
Though every nerve screams, "Leave this place" –
love counts for more than you would reckon.

There it stood, just silent wood, just bark beneath my hand;
I had not heard a single word! But rest assured: I understand.
I saw a tree the other day; its leaves were orange-red.
The strange resemblance laughed and played
strange tricks upon my feverish head ...

The Five Virtues

Peace, not ennui;
generosity, not cruelty;
beauty, not vanity;
faith, not dogma;
love, not fear.

Sonnet XLII (Question and Answer Session)

You say you love me, and then I protest.
I ask you why you want to hold my hand.
But everything you tell me would suggest
that logic just won't help me understand.
Love must just see beyond the obvious.
If so, it is like all the higher arts:
for any sculptured rock or piece of verse
is more than just the sum of all its parts.
But then, the merits with which I think you're blessed
are of that rarer kind few understand.
And I cannot explain, for I'm obsessed
and can't reply to logic's harsh demand.
And so we sit here, both wondering why;
we'll never know: love's ethereal as sky.

Blame it on the Curry

This is why I don't go out for Indian.
I didn't want to go out with you.
But I picked up the red silk napkin
and ordered the number 42:
the curry with the red sauce,
lamb and basmati rice.
And I'll tell you one thing, blue eyes
I couldn't handle the spice.
You're wondering where I was all night,
and I'll tell you true, my man:
I was in and out that beaded curtain
paying homage to the can.
And if you don't believe me, honey,
I'll tell you who you can blame.
Blame it on the curry, baby.
Blame it on the curry.

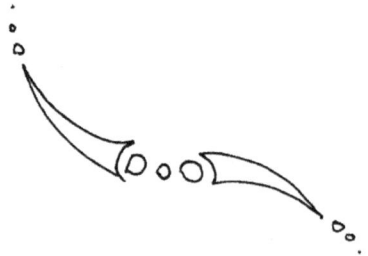

Laser Eye Surgery

The darkness follows me
leaving jagged footprints
but every time I turn around
to lay my hands on it
it has merely taken the shape
of a shadow

Life is clay, I have decided
I can mold it, smooth it, shape it
but what I can never figure out
is why it is still so soft.

Fear continues to argue with me
even though I have explained to it
how things are going to be around here.
So all that is left to do now
is merely stare it down
until it acknowledges me.

Come and find me
when you are ready to admit
that colors, and numbers, and shapes
are yours for the taking
and I'll give you leave to do it

In the meantime
the music will just have to stay
too loud for you.

Runaway

Standing in the headlights
of an oncoming car,
you can feel its gravity
for a split second: strong,
although infinitesimal against that
of the planet
(a corpulent orb with big hands
and a lachrymose eye.)

It starts out as an inanimate object of
subservient speed,
but all at once it becomes a thing of action
and massive, but subtle strength.
This pale stranger is a thing of beauty: it is
unique in this universe, and its bright eyes
catch mine.

I hear; I heed.
I dash to it, yearning for freedom from my snug cradle.
Do you understand (I inquire)
that you are my freedom,
you shall deliver me from the safe,
yet stifling
hold that this oversized planet has on me?
I feel it every time I lie in the grass
and gaze up at the stars,
and wholeheartedly desire
to escape.

Teetering on a single foot,
nearly toppled
by that omnipresent pull,

I wonder:
are these stars really so distant?
Such beautiful eyes, and yet
I am stuck here, rooted immobile in the gravity
of the grass.
The blades surround me.

So I dash toward freedom, and the car stops
for a split second,
and almost before
I can think, it speeds off,
carrying me away.
Independent of pull, oblivious to obligation.
So this is what I've been missing.

Verse on an Eleventh-Hour Homemade Valentine

I didn't buy you candy;
it's bad for you anyway.
And I can't afford a limousine,
not even for a day.

Red roses sure are pretty,
but their thorns hurt and then they die.
And cologne is downright dangerous.
What if that stuff got in your eye?

And so, instead of jewelry,
or underwear or wine,
my gift for you on Valentine's Day is ...
get this ... a Valentine!

Though it's mushy and it's gushy
and it's dripping with wet glue,
I hope you will forgive me –
it was the best that I could do.

So if all of that commercialism
gets under your skin,
please accept my humble love note
and the red envelope it's in.

Because it says I love you,
and that's all it needs to say.
Though I don't need a card to tell you,
or a special holiday.

So with this little token
I ask you to be mine:
won't you dust the glitter off your shirt
and be my Valentine?

No Onions

I ordered, for lunch, a burger,
and asked, "Please, on the side
could you bring me some of your onion rings,
most sumptuously fried?

"And also, while you're at it,
I'd like the burger with extra cheese.
And medium-well would sure be swell,
but ... NO onions, please."

The server, well, she was nice enough.
But she got a weird look on her face,
staring, fazed, with an eyebrow raised,
as though I were from outer space.

I pondered my server's reaction
as I paid and she made the change.
"This seems to happen a lot," I thought.
"Did I say something strange?"

"Why do we remember the past but not the future?"
~ Stephen Hawking

* * *

The Persistence of Memory

I see visions
of pennies on the ground
trees cut into decorative shapes
and guard dogs
in the doorway
and the inverse nostalgia
that I feel
at certain times of the day
a kind of pleasant anxiety about the future
has left me spent
to feel the former replaced by the
more recent
such a thing has led me
to call upon some of the more obscure areas
of my mind
in vain hopes of resurrecting the past
I hear answers that have no questions
except
in the end
who can you trust
but yourself

Flies on the Wall

If there were intelligent flies,
they would be highly paid spies.
They'd work for hire
by people who conspire
and be their ears and eyes.

Sonnet 9,846,524 (In All Honesty)

Sonnets are tricky; it takes awhile to make 'em.
But I figured I'd give it the college try,
'cause if someone didn't like it, you could take 'em.
So here's a love poem for my favoritest guy.
I guess I'll never know where you came from,
and I don't care, 'cause you're with me today.
I smile lots and lots now that you've come;
you're just that übercool. What can I say?
You're sweeter than a piece of pecan pie;
you make me happier than a Happy Meal.
When I'm with you, I feel like I could fly,
and you love me back, which just sweetens the deal.
And anyway, I don't need a fancy sonnet
to say this planet's better with you on it.

Philosopherphilia

Some look for truth in sacred texts, or on the temple walls,
and some in education, down ivory-tower halls.
Some look in fields of golden wheat, or follow a shining star,
but you answer all my questions, no matter how bizarre.

Some even look to oil stains. If you squint at asphalt right,
you'll see a marbled spectrum shine heavy in the starless night.
Though melancholy Gothic souls can find themselves therein,
I'll journey to your abode first if I am to begin.

Truth shows itself in weirdish ways, but I choose not to look
in heavy words of wizened men or pages of a book.
Though there are many places that the answers like to hide,
I think that I can find them all just walking by your side.

Song in Three Parts

I.
in this place of bloody power
elaborate shadows
pound my head
producing
the urge to scream

I swore I heard them say
do not think
let us beautify the dark shadows
of your mind
let us manipulate you
through the smooth picture of your television

maybe I will be happy
if I do this thing

II.
do you remember that night
crying from beneath
a black storm
we wrote iron music together

now
my brain thinks itself raw
hardening into sordid pictures

do you remember
I ached for you
with a power that finally tore free

III.
the moon whispers to me
let love warm
your diamond gardens
singing most delicate rose petals
do not let the dark essences play you

and so I envision
the cool moments that sweeten my days
peaches and sunlight
honey and mist

you see
my thoughts still flow
in the heady language of night
I trust these sayers of truth

and so I say
in my part of the sky
there is a purple star
shining for you

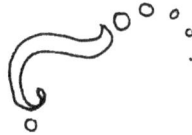

Heavy Metal Poisoning

Know thyself is a heady phrase.
Does it apply to runaways?
Can you see beyond the darkness
to the subtle glory of your days?

Confusion is a heavy thing.
It flies by night on shattered wing
and fills our heads with brooding doubt.
Silence your dark imagining.

Keep the demons in their cages;
lock them up for immortal ages.
Can you do it? I think you can.
Leave this time behind a hundred pages.

Black as night and crystal-hard,
each tear I shed was like a shard.
I loved you then but time has passed;
our lives go on, but leave us scarred.

The User

Use me up
wear me out
do me hard
or do without

And I
won't cry for
you

Push me down
mess me up
squeeze me out
into a cup

And I
won't die for
you

"The problem lies not in the stars, but in ourselves."
~ William Shakespeare

* * *

Diana's Lament

Bright Orion, save my soul –
descend from the starry heights.
Bring your dagger and your bow;
set the universe to rights.

Lord Orion, pure as flame –
archer with the shining eyes,
come again, as once you came,
to heal the pain, the wounds, the lies.

Sweet Orion, brave and true –
hunter of celestial might.
On humble knee I beg of you,
save me from the blinding night.

My Orion, though I see
your likeness in the northern sky,
you never shall return to me;
your home is in the heavens high.

Bright Orion, save my soul –
think of me, blind by day,
lost and lonely, far from whole,
until the stars shall carry me away ...

Bulletproof Hoodie

Woven of the finest nitrogen fiber
deflects any projectile
order one today
your 6D printer
can print it out
throw your trash in the hole
so there'll be some raw material
leftover synthesized food
some old socks
broken chair
the sunglasses you don't like anymore
and there you go
bulletproof hoodie
bullets are outlawed
but it might be cool
to have a hoodie that can deflect them
you never know

A Sweater of Knitted Brows

Learning the words
to a song no one knows
talking to a funeral dirge
in a serenade's clothes

I take only questions
and give only replies
an Achilles' heel
that cuts me down to size

And I'm making a sweater
of all these knitted brows
it hangs on pointed needle days
and was blocked with a cyanide douse

I wanted only mastery
and now I know too much
you ask me how to do it
and I can only blush

My age is marked by counting knots
I cannot sleep at night
and all I ask as I reach the end is
did I do it right?

Blessing

May you always have an old soul and a young heart
a bright future and faded jeans
a sweet smile and a bitter hatred of evil
many friends and few troubles
an easy burden and a tough skin.

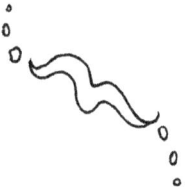

Rest Day

I've shut the computer down today.
I'm not ready for it, you see.
I've put my to-do list away –
it means nothing to me.

For today will be a rest day.
I knew it from the start.
A day to wander and to play –
some days that's just smart.

Even God rested on the seventh day,
so I'm not above a break.
Now I lay me down in bed,
a quick five to take.

Our brains work better rested.
They work while we do not.
So it's good for us to take time off,
and to do it a lot.

So if you see me chilling out,
I'm not wasting time.
My brain is searching on its own
for that perfect rhyme.

A Disadvantage of Frat Parties

There once was a guy from The Hague
whose head was shaped just like an egg.
When asked why his brain
was so round, he'd explain,
"I once got it stuck in a keg."

Thank You (2015)

to the police officer guarding the intersection at rush hour
to the barista at Starbucks
to the bus driver
to the server at the restaurant who kept my drink refilled
to the various men I don't know
who held the door for me
who let me on the bus first

but why oh why
did I forget to say it to my mom?

I Tried

I tried to write you a sonnet, my love,
but I couldn't get it right.
Could've used a muse to help from above,
but they all just laughed in spite.

I tried to write a fancy rhyme
about your eyes and hair.
But though I thought a lot, I couldn't find
rhyming words that fit anywhere.

I tried for a very long time to impale
some pentametric iambs
on the end of a pen that would write an email
you could read when you're tired of spam.

I tried to write you a sonnet, my dear,
but I found that it's really hard.
(Though it's fun to read ones that are by Shakespeare
in search of some help from the Bard.)

I tried to compose you a poem with form
and my failure wounded my pride.
So now, please allow me to stick to the norm
with assurance that I TRIED.

Beguiling

(inspired by The Beguiling of Merlin, *a painting by*
Sir Edward-Coley Burne-Jones,
with apologies to Edgar Allan Poe and his Raven)

Once upon a virgin forest,
Where the wrens and warblers chorused,
Traipsed a lovely, youthful maiden
With rich ribbons in her hair.
She had spent the morning walking,
With the deer and squirrels talking;
Laughing at the magpies' mocking,
She traversed the forest fair.
Running light and lithe and limber,
Fleetly crossed the forest fair,
Though her gentle feet were bare.

In that time no one recorded,
When kings over peasants lorded,
Woods were places of deep fear,
A danger to the unaware.
So therein no lass would ramble.
She might step on a magic bramble.
Each chose instead to pack her amble,
Wisely taking it elsewhere,
Wisely carting off her walk
And taking it away elsewhere.
But not this girl of red-gold hair.

Charmed brambles did not wake her worry,
Though they made other maidens scurry.
Nor, in fact, did any fearsome monster
That was hiding there.
Dragons' claws could not unnerve her;

Gryphons' cries would not perturb her.
Gorgon's heads did not disturb her
Placid spirit with that stare.
This youthful maiden of the forest was unmoved
By Gorgons' hair!
Such a thing is truly rare.

In truth, she brought no victuals with her,
As if she thought she could not wither
From the lack of nourishment that
Would her functioning impair.
Brought but a book, and just stood reading,
Stood there silent and unheeding
That her body might be needing
Soon to eat some filling fare.
In fact, this strange girl had no need
For any kind of human fare.
Her tome had all she needed there.

As the maiden stood there, waning
Not a bit, as she was gaining
Nourishment from every page
Her heavy volume wished to share –
Hark! What has appeared behind her?
Cloakèd mage in light to blind her,
Though its tone could not remind her
Of the sun's bright, holy glare.
His face had once been beautiful,
But now it bore a washed-out glare.
His cheeks and eyes were lined with care.

This wizened face had seen the world,
And now around it gently curled
Myriad thinning, brittle wisps
Of softly grayish wizard hair.

She turned her head with apprehension,
And met his gaze of rapt attention.
She saw his pale eyes lacked dimension,
Locked in a rather vacant stare.
She gazed unfazed, and unaffected
At that blank and slavering stare.
About his phlegm she did not care.

For the smiles her sweet lips smiled
Had much stronger men beguiled,
So she thought this aging wizard
Would nary a problem bear.
Thus, she started subtly grinning,
Thought her smile, winsome, winning,
Seemed to coax the faint beginning
Of a dawn from his blank stare.
As it was, his eyes stayed frozen
In their wide, unending stare,
In their dark and vacant stare.

She asked him why his watery eyes
Should wear that apathetic guise,
And not respond at least politely
To her smiling countenance fair.
He answered, with some irritation,
"I attempt a divination!
And to my growing consternation,
You don't even seem to care!
You just stand there, ignorant,
Not suffering and without a care!
I should just quit this grim affair."

She probed him further, quite demanding,
To increase her understanding:
His name and if there was a reason

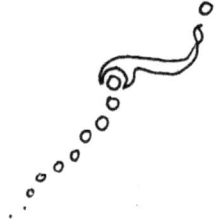

For his lying, hexing there.
"I am Merlin," he replied.
At her blank face he heaved and sighed.
"You mean my legends all have died?"
He asked, with melancholy air.
"I tell you, there was once a time
When stories of me filled the air.
But of these you seem unaware.

"And tell me how it is, O child,
That you stood and simply smiled,
Not affected even slightly
By the spell I cast. Do share."
And so she spent most of an hour
Telling him how magic power
Could touch her not, even the glower
Of a Gorgon's serpent-hair.
The wizard fought off sleep, and ran
His gnarled fingers through his hair –
Not a detail did she spare.

Prattling on about her mother,
Who birthed the girl and her twin brother,
Passing on a holy anti-curse
Of which she was the heir.
So the two of them were blessed,
Different from all the rest,
Able to withstand the test
The wizard was invoking there.
Her brother, too, was likewise blessed
With that bright shining red-gold hair.
But red locks he couldn't bear.

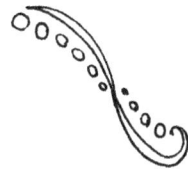

Merlin started feeling sorry
that he'd asked; his eyes grew starry.

As he thought about how far
He could escape away from there,
Suddenly his mind was cleared.
At once the grip of something weird
Took hold of him; it burned and seared,
And shook him as he languished there.
"O!" he cried, "my past has surely
Caught me in its deadly snare!
It bit me in the derrière!"

As the maiden gaped, he sighed;
As he explained, her eyes grew wide.
Now Merlin started to confide
A story of his own old care.
In his youth, the mage had sinned,
Thrown all caution to the wind,
When a lovely girl had grinned
At his thick, flowing red-gold hair.
"Alas," he sighed, "'tis now a mass
Of gray, and thinned from years of wear.
But I'd forgot the whole affair.

"Yet I, this day, am lounging, hexing,
And a child, reading, vexing,
Wakes in me the strange, perplexing
Thought that I might have an heir.
Did this woman have small hands?
Had she lived in many lands?
Had she an inn to keep large bands
Of travelers, off'ring beds and fare?"
"Yes to the three," the girl replied.
She dropped her book but not her stare.
It fell, remaining crumpled there.

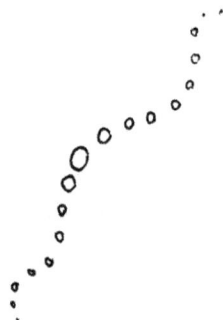

"So," he said, "I am a father
Of young twins, a son and daughter,
In whose veins there flows the blood
Of youth and life, immortal fare."
As Merlin spoke, he thought, alarmed,
That though his daughter's life was charmed
From magic, she could still be harmed
By mortal means. Was she aware?
He searched her face, but could not find
A whit of indication there.
He saw just her bemusèd stare.

She had no shield, nor magic fence,
No weapon for her own defense
From any form of violence
That might be befall her body fair.
With this thought the wizard crept
Closer; suddenly he leapt,
Seized the girl, and drew
A tiny dagger hidden off somewhere.
Drew from his robe a tiny knife
And killed the girl as she stood there,
Stood completely unaware.

From his robe he took a flask,
Hastening to a sordid task:
He quickly started filling
The small bottle with the fluid rare.
I know not what this dark man willed
For the blood which he had spilled,
But I do know that he filled
That bottle to the top out there,
Filled it to the brim and took
It off to some dark hidden lair.
Perhaps she is still lying there.

Brainchild

I pursue an infinite truth, but not here:
these clouds loom in a sky I wish were clear.
Surrounded by pre-rats in their fated race,
I likewise scurry toward a memory of your face.

Warm human blood pounds ruthlessly in my brain –
I hate this fragile flesh, this mortal pain.
I never thought that I could love a man,
a thing so alien, but I suppose I can.

I carry a dagger that I know can tear
the darkness which, like a fluid, seeps everywhere.
And you know surely that I'd never harm
a being, although mortal, similarly armed.

And all, and all, I think as I traverse
these ivory halls, is that it could be worse.
For though I struggle vainly in my trap,
in this, my foreign country, you're the map.

Beautiful Dreamer

Though I know I should be sleeping,
thoughts of you are lurking, creeping,
in the most secluded corners
of my psyche's darkest halls.
And the pen whose onyx ink
forms the thoughts that I shall think
scrawled these verses that you read
upon my brain's most salient walls.

For though it lacks my mind's permission,
my heart of hearts can't shake the vision
of your stone-slack body draped
haphazardly across a chair.
And I suppose it's just as well,
though my soul might rot in Hell
because this evilly pleasant thought
will accompany me there.

As I lay me down to sleep,
I pray this memory to keep,
so that I may recall the way
I saw you at your most relaxed.
That is the way we all should be,
in sacred idle, slumber holy.
We cannot reach enlightenment
with brain and body overtaxed.

When soon I join you in your rest,
calm your heart within your breast.
I wish that you remain at peace
so that I might regard you so.
Because our beauty shines most bright
when Spirit leaves to grace the night.
And the beauty of your sleep
is a bright magic you shall never know.

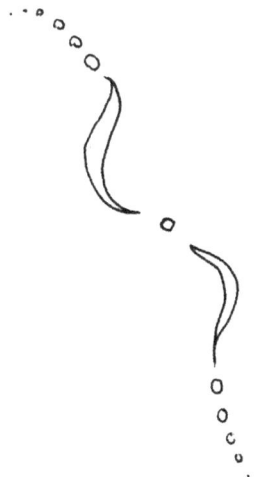

False Nature Haiku

False nature nearby
like mulch, pruned trees, flower beds,
mowed lawns, AstroTurf.

Panic of Life

"Do something that scares you every day" –
don't know who said that phrase.
But when Life scares me with its if,
and fear permeates my days,

I look about in desperation.

And all I can see is a comedian of a God
(a phrase stolen from Voltaire)
who's eyeing me with grim distaste,
who's stripped my wires bare –
and I am too afraid to laugh,
so I just walk down the street
with every step a slash,
and every word a prayer.

Shades of Blue

I cried when they gave my cat away
I've stayed up all night to greet the day
watching the last of the midnight fade
dissolving the last star

I've curled up in dark corners sighing
just because I feast while others are dying
I've seen the blue of this world in its every shade
because I know how many there are

I've watched my brothers and sisters run
I've seen human beings kill for fun
I walked miles and miles to learn this trade
no one's ever come this far

I've hidden under the bed when I should be smiling
felt the cold on my cheek from porcelain tiling
I spoke to the One who all the earth made
and I always raise the bar

I've asked for more than I deserve
was told you can have it if you're willing to serve
so I agreed and got no accolade
for the role I played in the war

Bus Driver's Break

Wheeled box, clunky and huge
sits, tempting me with its diesel fumes
I want to ride
to fly
but I can't
until he gets back.

Txt Msg

vry mchly i lv u
a clarion call 4 a dyng age
my gramr is por
but my wrds ring tru
lik goldn brds in a gilded cage

Blood Diamonds

Shiny rocks in golden rings
fit for the fingers of gods and kings.
But these diamonds that rich men hold so dear
are sold for pain and blood and fear.

They're dug from mines in far-off places,
found by men with haggard faces.
Stones shined up and used to buy
weapons of war and ways to die.

Tortured and beaten within inches of life,
do the miners know their stones can also buy a wife?
And the cruelty and horror doesn't reach the fore.
You won't hear about it in a jewelry store.

Do men know about this when they choose
diamonds for the women they plan to abuse?
Or that the stones passed down through generations
come with neuroses and frustrations?

The irony is profound and great,
but most people hear about it much too late.
The damage is already done,
for civil wars are never really won.

If I marry, I'll choose a rhinestone instead,
and let a shrink heal the pain inside my head.
For I know that no matter what it takes
we must forgive ourselves for our parents' mistakes.

Through an Angel's Eyes

you have bodies
torn to pieces
cut by fate
and by choice
you etch pictures of power
into your skin
beauty comes through pain
and some of you want more beauty
you tear your faces to bits
when life hasn't done it
enough for you
you survive though your home
is in tatters
you have lives
angels only have the afterlife
you have offspring
you create
you were made in God's very image
angels were made in your image
we are not like you
yet we are
you are given at birth the greatest gift God has to offer
free will
to do with what you wish
under God's law
even the most vicious sinners are pardoned eventually
but each who sins
is punished according to his sin
an eternity is relative to humans
your days are numbered
but you don't know how many you have
until they run out
you have hours, too

but they may last forever
particularly rush hours, lunch hours, happy hours, dying
hours
an eternity in Hell
is not necessarily a bad thing
if it happens
on the physical plane
and trust me
you don't want to be punished for your misdeeds
out here.
it is worse.
the DMV
office cubicles
bad restaurants
and the like
are great for punishing mild sinners
God is not evil
he is just
and as you might say
he has a wicked sick sense of humor
we are envious of you.
we want to be grimy too
we glow with holiness
we know God's love like you know the way to the grocery
we wear our halos and wings as you wear T-shirts and
jeans
but this is old hat to us.
we are like you but not
we look like you
yet we do not see like you.
you see reality.
we see spirituality.
you come in two genders
we are at once male and female, androgynous
you are held down by gravity

we are held aloft by spirit
you live in perpetual hope that your pain will be cleansed
when you perish
and reach heaven
and we live in faith that we will grow in humanity
as we fulfill our assignments
and protect, nurture, guide, inspire, and inform humans.
we are there for you in your hour of direst need.
and we and God are like THAT.
we aren't limited in our vision, you are
but we are limited by what you can see
if that makes any sense
so as they say
don't drive faster
than your guardian angel can fly

Soul Traveler

she came home the other day
got in my personal space
and when I looked in the mirror
I didn't see my face.

she's sad, she's crying jagged tears
she wants to board the plane
but I'm so glad to see her
and have her home again

she's agreed to stay a while
before taking off again
and she promises that if she leaves
she'll leave a note to explain

it's useful when your soul is there
it gives your words more weight
so the next time she is back in town
I'll meet her at the gate

The Zen of Zen

Today I will be
the bee on a flower
with the flower in your hair
and your hair down your back
and your back to the sun
and the sun in the East
and the East right where it should be.

"Just when you thought that things could not get any bet-
ter for DeSmet pitcher Bob Keppel, they did when he got a
call from the New York Mets Monday afternoon. ... Keppel
actually received the news of his spot in the draft from the
Internet before he heard it from anyone else. 'I heard it on the
Internet first,' Keppel said. 'I knew I was a Met then. I got a
phone call from the Mets about five minutes after I saw it on
the Internet.'"
~ Jeff Paur, the *St. Louis Post-Dispatch*

* * *

Bob Keppel

There once was a guy from DeSmet
who got drafted to be a Met.
They called him at home,
but he'd already known –
he found out on the Internet.

"Who is this 'they' people are always talking about?"
~ my dad

* * *

The Hierarchy of Erratic Yodelers

t.h.e.y. ought to fix the leaky pipes in the apartment complex
t.h.e.y. are always annoying me with their loud music downstairs
t.h.e.y. didn't salt the roads enough last time it snowed
t.h.e.y. raised the taxes again
the Hierarchy of Erratic Yodelers
screw with us every way they know how
and they're always yodeling
at random times
some are above in the hierarchy
some are below
some are in between
but
t.h.e.y. gave me a raise
t.h.e.y. put me next to the cute guy in class
t.h.e.y. managed to get this great law passed
t.h.e.y. found my dog
the Hierarchy of Erratic Yodelers
get us the good stuff on a platter
and they're always yodeling
at random times
some are above in the hierarchy
some are below
some are in between
and
t.h.e.y. just kinda stand there and stare
t.h.e.y. are pretty much the same every day
t.h.e.y. try and try and just get nowhere
t.h.e.y. are always watching and never doing anything

the Hierarchy of Erratic Yodelers
never ever change
and they're always yodeling
at random times
some are above in the hierarchy
some are below
some are in between
the Hierarchy of Erratic Yodelers

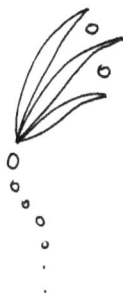

Stopping by the Bar on a Friday Evening
(With apologies to Robert Frost)

Whose beer this is, I think I know.
He left it on the table, though.
He will not see me stopping here
To steal a sip before I go.

My other friends must think it weird
When I have my own drink near.
I mean, why would I dare to take
A swig of someone else's beer?

One gives her ponytail a shake
To ask if there is some mistake.
And I, I don't let fly a peep,
But change my mind: I am no snake.

The mug is lovely, dark and deep.
But what I sow, I always reap,
And I've already got a heap
Of bad karma that did not come cheap.

On Hearing That My Father, a Navy Reservist, Was Being Called to Active Duty

I heard the awful news today.
You're being called to war.
Do they know that this could be the end
of the father I adore?

You're too old, and anemic;
your hair is going gray.
But I could never see myself
begging you to stay.

Maybe I could pull a Mulan;
sometimes hard thoughts fill my head
of taking up your M-16
and going in your stead.

But I could never do it.
I'm too much the pacifist.
Our father who art in warrior's garb,
you will be sorely missed.

And I'm plagued with troubling visions
of your body lying on the sand.
I hope you know what you're doing –
I'll never understand.

Alligator Personal Ad

I was reading the Miami Herald one day,
when I noticed a personal ad
that stood out from all the rest
although it was just as bad.

An alligator had written it, and
I'm not sure what he had to gain
by writing "Green gator seeks cold-blooded lady
who likes long walks in the rain.

"I like vacations in the Everglades,
hunting, and sharpening my claws.
But not making out – it's awkward, you see
because of the shape of my jaws."

I'd turn down any gator that hits on me,
no matter how much he begs.
I mean, if we decided we wanted kids,
would I start laying eggs?

"The reasonable man adapts himself to the world; the unreasonable man persists in trying to adapt the world to himself. Therefore all progress depends on the unreasonable man."
~ George Bernard Shaw

* * *

The Jerk's Revenge

It is said that the reasonable man
adapts as best he can
to the ravaging whims
of the world around him,
but progress he can't understand.

Now the jerk, on the other hand,
(a.k.a. the unreasonable man),
will refuse to adapt,
so deserves to be slapped.
But all progress is at his command.

Cereal Killer

There is a part of me
who believes a midnight snack should only be eaten at twelve.
He sighs, casts red-rimmed eyes
at the misshapen cereal pieces,
unmeasured milk.
He points out that it's thirty-nine minutes too early.

Of all the voices in my head,
this one is the most direct. He needs
a task to occupy him, he tells me.
"There is a chip in the bowl,"
he says.

I try to subdue him with the complex problems of
midnight metabolism,
simple carbohydrates,
partially hydrogenated soybean oil.

He is still not satisfied,
but allows me to resume the task at hand,
watching with distaste as I gratefully ingest the sugar
that will fuel a few more hours
of creation.

Omega Song

The brilliant fire when the day is done
is also a sign to everyone
That the day is over and the night has begun.
Sing derry, sing ho.

The frenzied spinning of a top
belies the fact that soon it will drop,
whirling and twirling 'til it slows to a stop.
Hai, diddly hy-o.

When a child is born, the tear in its eye
and the plaintive pain of its infant cry
serves as a warning that one day it will die.
Sing bright like the sun.

The billowing flame they call desire
eventually slows to a gentler fire
'til there's just embers left from that once-great pyre.
Now my song is done.

Alternate Ending for Romeo and Juliet

I see her gentle visage scarred with doubt.
O, would that she would let her secret out.
It pains mine heart to see her grieve this way
About the youth whose life has fled this day.
O'er his limp form she stood with dagger point
Held o'er her breast, as if she would anoint
The granite altar upon which he lay
With blood spilled for true love, and then there stay!
'Twas happy that the lord, the lady fair,
And I arrived in time to see her there,
And save her from the weapon in her hand.

Now there is peace and hope throughout the land,
For every Capulet and Montague
Did all hatred and enmity eschew
When they heard of the death of Romeo.
And yet, the little maid is pining so.
It seems as if she holds within her heart
Some agony with which she cannot part.
I wish that I could help her pain abate,
But as a holy man I can but wait
Until she brings her secret care to me,
So that the grace of God can set her free.

But soft – she enters now my secret place,
And seats herself, all full of youthful grace.
"Dear Friar," she begins in quavering tones,
"There is a melancholy in my bones.
I went to mourn within a hidden glen,
But I was followed there by seven men!
I wish to live a chaste life evermore,
But I cannot with suitors at the door."
Is Juliet so wise beyond her years,

Or is her sorrow merely wanton tears?
I cannot tell; her grieving might be pure.
I would fain ask the girl just to be sure.

"Then Romeo, for whom you had such love,
Is not forgotten like a misplaced glove?
He was, in fact, not but a childish whim?
You would not marry just for love of him?"
"There is no man," she says, "in all this land,
To whom I would consent to give my hand.
Good Friar, I do not know what to do.
How can I to his memory be true,
When lords and princes follow me about?"
I ask her, "Do you know without a doubt
That you would rather live a purer life
And that you never wish to be a wife?
For if this is the choice that you have made,
Then I will – so help me God – come to your aid."

She does not speak, but in her eyes there gleams
The light of gratitude, or so it seems.
So I tell Juliet about a place
In which I know she can sure hide her face.
A man's heart would be melting but to see
The joy she shows at that word, "nunnery".

But as she makes her brief polite adieu,
I ask the child what she fain would do.
At that she leaves my sanctum silently.
But at the door, she turns and looks at me.
No man hath lived, except the Christ perchance,
Who could divine the meaning of that glance.
For even I, a Friar with training full,
Still find her haunted gaze unfath'mable.
And with that look she flees my wond'ring sight.
If what I hear be true, she left that night.

For twenty-seven years I have not heard
From her, and of her whereabouts, no word.
And so, as here I sit with pen in hand,
I write to every convent in the land.
But I have not located as of yet
A sister by the name of Juliet.

The Hardest

An aged man,
though he still stands strong.
His parents taught him
right from wrong.

A God-fearing man,
he walked the line
between doing good
and feeling fine.

A hardworking man,
he fixed locks on doors.
As an Army Reservist,
he fought in three wars.

A family man,
he raised nine kids,
crying when three of them
closed their lids.

So I asked him,
"When push comes to shove,
what is the hardest thing you've done?"
He smiled and said, "I fell in love."

Rondo Alla Turca
(inspired by the piece of the same name by Mozart)

Throw away the hate and pain;
let's all go dancing in the rain!
Do a bouncy pirouette,
even though your feet are wet.
Those who say life's a disease
have never danced the ivory keys.
Sing a happy nonsense song –
Mozart, Mozart all day long.
Dance and dance and dance some more,
sing until your lungs are sore.
Life just isn't life unless
lived with giddy happiness.
Amid the static noise and haste,
leap and spin and eat the paste.
When life tries to give you lemons,
dance the Rondo with the demons!
If life's box step feels too placid,
Mozart's like a waltz on acid.
Squeeze the raindrops from your hair:
water, water everywhere!
Toss aside each boundary;
dance a dance that's wild and free.
You can feel the *joie de vivre*,
if you catch the Mozart fever!
Twirl and whirl upon your toes;
follow where the music goes!
Dance your dance into the night;
tiptoe down the black and white.
Even when there's no more rain,
we'll still dance away life's pain.
Hop and skip and jump and leap.
Never grovel, crawl or creep.

At life's crossroads, make a choice.
Keep your peace or RAISE YOUR VOICE!
Why stay in your staid mazurka
when you can Rondo Alla Turca?!

Magnetic Poetry: The Fridge IV

* * *

television
rusts the iron in my blood
and I come away with
a need to sleep

* * *

in the end
who can you trust
but yourself

* * *

you are
warm peaches and milk
in the morning
forest leaves
after a rain
to me
you will always be beautiful

* * *

sometimes in dreams
I swim through
diamond waters
under a purple moon

* * *

beneath this skin
petals harden into rock

Home

the Earth came home today
and cried elaborate tears
when she saw
her gown like gardens
delicate with years

Strawberry Crush

well call me nuts on a stick with extra crazy sauce
but I've seriously got it bad
wiggly skin, hairs standing on end
all the usual signs
weave a map
hung on the wall
of some foreign country
that never existed before
but it's so familiar
the lights are brighter
my pack is lighter
I'm no fighter
but I've practically got to hold myself down
I know what to look for
and everything I see
has led me to come to the conclusion
that that new music I was going to listen to this weekend?
will have to wait
God I can't even remember
what I came downstairs for
anymore
doesn't matter...
hey I'll call you up
and we'll talk about nothing whatsoever
and maybe you can tell me again about that thing
that you told me about seventeen times already
I don't care
it's not every day
you get to dance with someone
other than your own demons

doodling hearts in notebooks
I laced my sneakers with pink
just for the hell of it
even though I hate pink
I've got me a strawberry crush
but don't worry about me
it's all good
you want to come over in two minutes?
fair enough
you don't have to tell me twice
I wasn't expecting you to say that
but I wasn't expecting you to say anything
when I saw you
and suddenly got the urge to flirt
even though I'd never done such a thing before
it's a language I never learned to speak
although I've tried
I hope you like my hair
it took me all day
to get it to look this haphazard

Lost Pen

"Hey, Lloyd," I said.
"What's on your mind?"
"A violent, bloody hatred
for all humankind."
"What's the matter,
malware on your PC again?"
"No, Larry in Accounting
stole my blue pen."
"Let's go get it," I said.
"We'll be back before lunch.
Bet it's sitting on his desk.
I just have a hunch."
So we took the stairs
to the Accounting floor.
Larry's cube's on the right,
next to the door.
He was on the phone
with our co-worker Ben.
When he finished, Lloyd poked him,
asked about his blue pen.
"Oh, I lent it to Molly."
(The CEO's secretary.)
When we asked her, she said
she gave it to Barry.
So we headed back up
to the Marketing floor.
Barry said that he dropped it
on the floor.
So we poked around
under desks and chairs,
and finally found Lloyd's pen
next to the stairs.
So I asked, "What'll you write
now that you've got your pen back?"
He shrugged and said,
"You know, I'll just use black."

Oasis – a haiku

A wet leaf hangs low
and gives the dry earth a drink
with its fallen drop.

The Disneyland Stamp Girl Meets Her Match

When you go to Disneyland,
they stamp your hand.
So if you want to leave
and come back, you can.

There's a girl at the gate
with the stamp at her command,
and no one comes back in
without a stamp on their hand.

So one day she was stamping
and it was all going grand,
until a man with no hands
came to Disneyland.

She was struck with confusion.
What should she do?
Was there some sort of protocol
she could adhere to?

Saying, "May I stamp your stump?"
seems in very poor taste.
Like asking someone
if you can spit in their face.

She didn't know what to do,
so she just stood, stamp in hand,
holding up the line of people
going to Disneyland.

So now, locked in an impasse,
forever they stand,
the Disneyland stamp girl
and the handless man.

Yesterday

Yesterday a girl grew up
and cried her last few tears,
dancing a little as she shed
the petticoats of years.

Today she laced her sneakers
and climbed a leafy tree,
grinning and laughing like a kid,
as wise as wise can be.

Be a Goth

Hitch a ride on the hearse and be a Goth,
come and join our ranks and be a social moth.
Come lurk in the shadows with the superior ones,
the artistic intelligentsia, the wise, loving sons
of the free who live in the home of the true.
If you need to belong, well, you know what to do.
You don't sign in blood; you'll find ink is just fine.
Buy it at our Goth shop for a buck sixty-nine.
You don't have to wear black, or be manic-depressive,
or worship the Devil, just be over-obsessive.
Wear leather or vinyl, and don't let it hang slack,
though that isn't a problem as long as it's black.
Put on buckles and boots, makeup and lace;
a Goth guy sees no harm in painting his face.
Buy a skirt, or a trench coat. It'll suit you, I promise.
And don't forget your tight black pajamas.
Heavy gloves ... colored hair ... such Gothly attire
any non-Goth poseur couldn't help but admire.
And if anyone threatens your way of life,
just put your ashen wrists under the knife.
'Cuz we don't kill ourselves over just anything,
only in protest if they won't let us bring
our very own special flavor to each city,
if they won't let us slouch and arouse their pity.
Because what we Goths stand for is a kind of ennui
you only find in America. Our lives sure suck, don't they?
We're more bored and lonely in the US of A
than any Afghan, Argentinian, Mongol or Malay.
We can never get enough MP3 players;
our cars and our clothes just won't answer our prayers.
So turn from religion and join our dark band.
We promise that, as a Goth, you'll find a cadaverous hand
which is that of a friend, who'll be yours 'til you die,

unless you conform to the masses (or try).
Oh, join up today if you're not a cretin,
if you think all conformists ought to be beaten,
if you're into anarchy (the new school definition),
if you're feeling depressed because you've been wishin'
for a place you can go where they all know your name
(whether "Darklord" or "Raven" it's all the same).
Join, and start dressing today in black leather.
Why be happy when we can be Goths together?

"'Do you know, I always thought Unicorns were fabulous monsters, too? I never saw one alive before!' 'Well, now that we have seen each other,' said the Unicorn, 'if you'll believe in me, I'll believe in you.'"
~ Lewis Carroll, *Through the Looking-Glass*

" ... Now I will believe
That there are unicorns, that in Arabia
There is one tree, the phoenix' throne, one phoenix
At this hour reigning there."
~ William Shakespeare, *The Tempest*

* * *

Believe

Oh, I believe in magic, and castles in the sky
and jeweled things with lacy wings and fairies fluttering by.
And I believe in satyrs, and magic spells and gnomes,
and fire-breathing dragons in their subterranean homes.
Yes, I believe in paintbrushes that paint the sunlit lands,
and I believe in elves that roam the earth in silent bands.
Oh, I believe in gypsy songs that conjure wondrous things,
and shiny golden apples, and gods and fairy kings.
And I believe in phoenixes, and animals that speak,
and which bestow their great rewards upon the kind and meek.
Oh, I believe in magic vines that envelop a castle,
and little men who can spin straw into a golden tassel.
And I believe in magic cloth that can detect a liar,
and I believe in goddesses alight with purple fire.
Yes, I believe in golden roads that lead to far-off places,
and I believe in the one good deed that all the bad erases.
And I believe in ancient runes, and pebbles that grant wishes.
I even believe in invisible hands that help to do the dishes.
Yes, I believe in the fount of youth, and immortality,
and I believe in the Holy Grail and knights and chivalry.
Oh, I believe in unicorns, and giants and wizards too,
and I even believe (believe it or not) that I believe in you.

Under Where?

I know it's the latest new style
and I'm doing my best not to stare
but I can't help but wonder if he knows
that the world can see his underwear?

If a gentleman follows the fashion
it's certainly his own affair
but I wonder if someone has told him
he's showing off his underwear?

Forgive me if I am not "with it"
but I'm guessing he just doesn't care
that his pants 'round his hips like he's wearing
is exposing his underwear.

Oops. He read my verse over my shoulder
and he thinks that I'm not being fair
and it's no business of mine how he dresses
and how he wears his underwear.

Well, if it were up to me all the young men
who wander the big world out there
would pull 'em up and cover their boxers or briefs –
that's why they call it *under*wear.

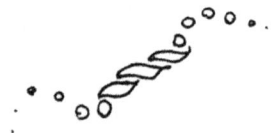

Fragments of Dreams

The morning light
shook me gently awake
leaving me with strange memories
they were brand-new, yet they seemed
to be of things that had happened ten years ago
cobwebby, like the memories
had been in my head
for years.
When did all this happen?
I asked myself
half-asleep
and wondering
was that a dream?
About the things that were a bit more realistic
or did it really happen?
The more the day became alive
the less I remembered
until all that was left
were a few fragments
of dreams

Cutter

I slice my skin
to feel the pain
would I could make scars
whole again

A Thousand Times

If you've told me once
you've told me a thousand times
but not in so many words
I can't remember quite what you said
but I remember it was something along the lines of
I'm dumb
I'm obnoxious
I'm mean
I'm hard
I'm alone
I hate you.
Now granted
as I've said
you never actually said any of that
but it was written
all over your tone
your voice
your body language
and my face, I'm sure
which is why you screamed at me
to leave.
Bye

The Ship That Did Trade With the World: An Allegory

There once was a ship of dreams, they say,
That carried a cargo of bright midday.
And its masthead sported a robed woman distorted
On its prow so incredibly free.

Resilient sails from its crossbeams hung
While the crewmen sang hale in their breathless tongue,
And the pitch in its seams shone like onyx gleams
As it sliced through the open sea.

No barnacles ever adorned its wood;
No mildew made it less than supremely good.
But there were those who stated that they truly hated
Every whit of that damnable craft.

They were eaten with envy at the joy of the crew,
Whose load was lighter than what they themselves knew.
So they hatched out a scheme to end the dream
Of that sloop from heaven staffed.

With its tricolored standard caressed by the breeze,
The ship set sail for a voyage of ease.
But the sun in the sky had not yet reached its high
When the dissidents stormed the deck.

They tore down the sails and the twin masts too,
Killing a great many of the crew.
By the time the great Dipper lit the crippled clipper,
It was held by black knights in check.

The remaining crew, incensed by the loss,
Appealed for revenge to their boss.
That was last century. We can plainly see
That captain was less than wise.

For the sloop was well-armed with cannonballs to spare:
Enough for one for every man there.
Their flight was straight, and their power great,
But precision was lost to size.

They aimed for the arid, troubled lands
That they believed quartered the men by whose hands
The attack was made. And by Jove, they paid
Back every horrible freak,

Every last landlubber lurking there.
(There was no way to know exactly where
Any higher mind who was behind
The attack hid; they killed both the strong and the weak.)

Now, in this day and age we know this tale
To be false, like the legend of Jonah's whale.
Never could there ever be such a fool
To lead a crew of angels to be so cruel.

Magnetic Poetry: The Fridge II

should I stop in the place of stars
beneath some blue garden
in a sea of shadows

* * *

  we will sit
you and I
whisper or cry
  in a tongue of delirious worship
  I never trust
those god-like men

* * *

love can ease Mondays
  be like sweet water
let life be free
and do for you
what nothing else could

* * *

sweating under a hard sun
his language trudges
as on flooded roads
toward art

* * *

beautiful boy
swimming through moments
    so delicate
    sad as twilight rain

* * *
    shall this
     cold knife
      still the winds
or rip away
    the heat of bitterness

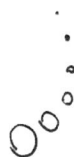

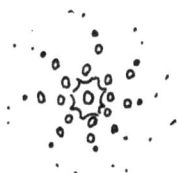

The Find

Went out at dusk to catch fireflies.
Couldn't help thinking
about how they seduce their mates:
leaping up occasionally
with their sudden flashes of brilliance.
They do it best at twilight.

Came out with my jar,
fashioning a cool Morse lantern
with a hole for each tiny breath –
the most important part of the sport.

Held up my catch to the west,
watching them speak
to the glow of distant lightning,
blue on blue.
Closed my eyes,
holding back a shiver.
Thought that when God
was giving out souls,
He gave them to fireflies too.

When

my brain knows languages I do not and it hurts
dark blossoms sing in this room
and you understand my glance better than all the men
I never knew
this is all I have to give you at the moment
signs saying "feed me" are everywhere
but I cannot read them
dancing in the night is one of the courses we offer
try it, you'll like it
I'm down to earth, you know
and that's not all I have to say about that
five six seven eight
as you've been taught music starts from the top
there's snow there
it's lonely at the top
but they know me here
I'm a known quantity
so it's not difficult
to figure me out
horses of all colors
ask me with their eyes,
when?

Monopoly

Several years ago, in 2120,
companies were making too little money.
There were too many brands to confuse a buyer;
they were lowering prices and refusing to hire.
Finally, there ensued an out-and-out war.
It became an adventure just to go to the store.
Soon, just one brand was left – it survived all the wars.
What was this brand? Norka®, of course!

It had been a small name 'til the big ones departed.
But they fought each other, leaving home turf unguarded.
And we Norka® execs, being shrewd,
pounced right away like piranhas their food.
So before anyone knew it, our plan was unfurled:
Norka® brand was the ONLY brand in the world!
But Norka® means quality. That's never been news.
Only now, it's much simpler. You don't have to choose.

The airwaves are filled with our Norka® ads;
we are in control of all the fads.
"With Norka® brand sneakers, you'll be a trendsetter!
The Norka® brand: there just ain't nothin' better."
If you go to the store, all you will see
is Norka® brand products for you and me!
Like...

Norka® brand lasers, Norka® brand kites,
Norka® brand pillows for pillow fights.
Norka® brand bicycles, Norka® brand plastic,
Norka® dictionaries for being bombastic.
Norka® brand tissues, Norka® brand pens,
Norka® brand underwear (women's and men's).
Norka® brand chocolate and almond bark,

Norka® brand night-lights for use in the dark.
Please your man with a Norka® brand thong!
(But you might get sued if you spell Norka® wrong.)

Norka® brand cellophane, Norka® brand bread,
Norka® brand hats to wear on your head.
Norka® brand cookies, Norka® brand cake,
Norka® erasers fix every mistake.
Norka®, not Pepcid, to take when you hurl,
Norka®, not Godiva, to give to your girl.
Norka® brand sunscreen and Norka® brand flowers,
Norka® air freshener that lasts for hours!
Norka® brand mirrors, Norka® brand punch,
Norka® brand brown sacks for packing your lunch.
(We might have kind of a funny name,
but that doesn't matter with this kind of fame.)
Our list of products stretches to the sky.
You can't escape; don't even try.

(This didn't really happen. Consumers still have a voice.
So buy Norka® products NOW, while there's still a choice...)

Thank You (2001)

For a gift whose substance was greater
than the harried passers-by probably suspected.
They couldn't have seen
the brief electricity that crackled in contact,
hand-to-hand,
heart-to-heart.

For the two sacred offerings of folded paper
given in passing,
and received by a soul made grateful by desperation.

For the tiny crane and the four-petaled flower
whose delicate creases renewed my faith in humanity
and which, but for the familiar blue lines,
may as well have been carved alabaster:
so much
did I treasure them.

For a gift given without ceremony
to a trembling recipient
overwhelmed by passion and pain.

For the poignant truth that came
when they were placed into my cupped hands,
but surely with the thought
that even deep truths
have a shallow end.

For all this I thank you.
I left them on the windowsill.

Drugged My Drink

Didn't you. I know
I feel super weird for some reason
and it's gotta be something bad
that you slipped me. Right?
Okay no, you say
it's just you
and I say well,
is it warm
in here
or is it just me?

Nice

What would I do
without the voices in my head?
I don't know.
I think I'll ask them.

Sometimes they tell me I have the gift
to envision dreams like hard symphonies,
to make the world what it needs to be:
Black.
For I am the darkness,
melancholy made manifest.

For this was I born.
That is what they say.
And I whisper
no,
for the means of my death
is my own business.

But I remember yesterday
and everything I screwed up
and I am drunk in a dream world
and I have to come onstage
and accept the stupid award.

And I am incapacitated
incompatible
incomprehensible
indefensible
and I die a couple of times
and the voices say, come back.

They are good.
But they whisper lies of power.
Worship the shadow gods, they tell me.
I will.
I won't.
You will cut off my wings.
You are beautiful.
You will be my demise.
You will save me.
And the cat and dog duke it out in my head.
And sometimes, the bad guy wins.

It is these days that I become a typo,
the sausage on the pizza for someone who hates sausage,
a dancer with no feet,
the snot in a little kid's nose,
the crud at the bottom of a garbage can,
the spinach on the salad bar of life.

Sometimes I lose.
It is on these days that God tells me
it's okay, he grades on a curve.
And I humor him
and tell him
I'll try again.
And he smiles.
And I think to myself, this guy is kind of weird
while he makes us ice cream galaxies with hot fudge,
and we chill out
until the Armageddon.
And he lets me come back
and he says, you can have faith in me.
I have faith in you.
And I say, Nice.

Will I

When I have died,
don't bury me in my best clothes.
I never wore any of that stuff, anyway.
Put me in jeans from the thrift store,
and a T-shirt with something on it about art.
No – better yet, deck my body
in some of the motley clothes
I made myself,
put together with my own hands
so I didn't have to conform to
the way the world is shaped.

When I have died,
don't sing sad songs.
I never liked that, anyway.
I say, why sing if you don't sing happy?
Let them all dance light,
everyone who has a piece of my heart.
I never saw any reason not to be happy,
and I still don't.

When I have died,
don't say prayers over my body.
I never believed any of that stuff, anyway.
Recite the poems I loved,
sing some of the songs I collected,
share the things I wrote
while I lived.

When I have died,
don't stash my carcass in a box.
I never lived like that, anyway.

Burn my remains on a pyre
laid with flowers,
and spread the ashes everywhere I never could get to.
Australia,
France,
Hawaii.

When I have died,
don't cry for me.
I never did that too much, anyway.
Tell jokes and rhyme rhymes,
make puns and play games.
Sing and dance and live your lives with the relish
with which I lived mine.

When I have died,
don't cover my face with makeup.
I never hid it with that stuff, anyway.
Leave it plain, no masks,
like I showed it to the world.
Let whoever would see me see me as I am,
artless, guileless.

When I have died,
remember the things I lived for.
I won't remember any of it, anyway.
Keep me in your heart;
tell my story while you tell yours.

·˙·ₒₒ₀◊°°ₒ ·

Beach

The tide was low when I awoke;
the sea was draining from the shore.
It laid its life upon the sand:
bright shells the creeping sea-things wore.

I rushed to join the rushing surf.
I bounded out, naïve, unshod,
to play and gather treasures there,
temptations of a fickle god.

I scurried this way, hurried that.
Each piece of sea-polished glass,
new shell, or piece of driftwood
was prettier than the last.

Presently the sun grew dimmer,
sank to the horizon line.
And in the dark I could not see.
I'd have to leave this beach of mine.

With that I ran much faster still,
with all that I could hold.
I filled my pockets, filled my bag
with stuff worth more to me than gold.

The tide was high when I returned,
no time to see it all.
So I sought the protection
of the dark stone seaboard wall.

My knees buckled in despair.
Such things beyond my reach!
My heart dissolved: I'd spent the day
exploring but a single beach.

But as I dragged my cargo in,
one thing I realized:
you can't take it with you.
But you can take your eyes.

Sing a Song of Silence

Sing a song of silence
to hide the spreading stain
four and twenty shrouded souls
in fresh untainted pain
when the door was opened
I stared in disbelief
for my heart was never stolen
but here I'd found the thief.

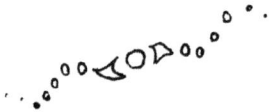

Magnetic Poetry: The Fridge I

though the mornings be cold
   my heart is like   a   warm   sea

* * *

music sings blue power
  in an   elaborate suit

* * *

   soft arms left that boy
feeling so delirious
       he could swim above stars

* * *

some still think
   tiny diamond kittens
   in the language of sky
trust those sayers of truth

* * *

when   car lights whiten the road
   will we watch from under   rocks

Philophobia

My greatest fear is to die by fire,
to burn to death in a hungry pyre,
wailing helpless as the bright flame sears –
yes, this is one of my greatest fears.

I really dread being killed by a fall,
to plummet from a building with a thousand-foot wall,
the ground rushing toward me in such a hurry –
yes, falling has always plagued me with worry.

I'm terrified of death by the knife,
to be brutally stabbed in the prime of life,
writhing in pain as I return to the dust –
yes, I'm really afraid of that fatal thrust.

My greatest fear is to die by love,
to be pecked to death by that rabid dove,
and have my entrails thrown every which way –
but it can't be that bad if it happens every day.

Elemental, My Dear

My love is a love like the fire, my dear;
it will warm you and light your way.
If you always stay near, you have nothing to fear
from the flame that burns in my heart, my heart,
from the flame that burns in my heart.

My love is a love like the earth, my dear;
it will guard you and give you strength.
Roam wherever you will, it will be there still,
like the ground that lies under your feet, your feet,
like the ground that lies under your feet.

My love is a love like the water, my dear;
it will calm you and quench your thirst.
It will lull you to sleep with songs peaceful and deep,
like the river that flows to the sea, the sea,
like the river that flows to the sea.

My love is a love like the air, my dear;
it will touch you and fill you with joy.
Though you can't see it there, you'll know it's everywhere
by the wind that blows through the trees, the trees,
by the wind that blows through the trees.

My love is a love elemental, my dear,
like the four that make up this world.
Even if it should perish, my love would still flourish,
like the fire, earth, water and air, and air,
like the fire, earth, water and air.

Summernightthoughts (With Cat)

    Sweet dark
sweet cat
  street cat   hiss cat
  house cat   hiss
  fuzzycat tame cat
    with claws.
 Yellow eyes   slits   ears flick
  in the dark
in the jungle of a plush rug.
  Prettycat   fuzzy cat plush
  solid ball of purr
    fur
easy gray with hints of white
      moonlight
shines
   in the dark night
  cascading through the window
   glows   silver-white.
 Turn right
 step over the cat (purr)
 chirp of a cricket
  in the   east
 buzzing of bugs   horizon-bourne buzz
insects buzzing   fuzzycat purring
  summernightthoughts whirring
to the tune of a distant   dance   chance upon
  a brain-born
jewel

To the World

I figured that if they really
wanted it kept closed,
like they said,
they would have locked it
or threatened my death
or something.

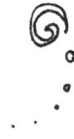

It wasn't really my fault anyway.
Because after all,
they're the ones
who gave it to me in the first place.

How was I supposed to know
that inside were all the demons that plague humanity?

It wasn't my fault.
But they're making me write this,
so I'm sorry.
(But it wasn't my fault)

~ Pandora

The Story

Once upon a time
there was a girl
who loved to tell stories.
She wouldn't shut up
but nobody minded
because she told the best stories
anybody had ever heard.
Everyone smiled to hear them.
They healed people's pain
made them feel things they'd never felt before
let them walk in other people's shoes
let them dance when they couldn't even walk
let them fly when they didn't even know
there was a sky.

But one day
the girl was bored.
She said, "I'm bored.
So I'm gonna write the best story there ever was."
So she did.
But all of her friends, who are real characters anyway
ended up as the characters in this story.
And the world fell apart
and everyone lost their marbles
and they were rolling all over the floor
people were tripping over them and falling
picking up other people's marbles by accident
and everything really sucked.
So she said, "Oops
I'll fix it"
And she did.
And they all lived happily ever after
well mostly anyway
and the girl said "I think maybe I won't write any more stories...
unless I can't resist."

The End

Missing

I didn't like the setup
didn't like the situation
a coupling built on pain
and miscommunication

of all the colors of my heart
right now I feel dark blue
I didn't even like you much
but right now I'm missing you.

Caveat

You're altogether too close, sometimes
whispering in my ear
in a voice like oiled honey.
Easy – those lightning bolts shooting down the wires of my back
might make me glow.
Then they'd know.

You're altogether too gallant, sometimes
with your unconscious habit
of holding the door for me.
Watch out – the rough façade you wear might start to crack
when you're with me.
Then they'd see.

You're altogether too gentle, sometimes
tempering your strength
to hold me tenderly.
Careful – the loving side you think you lack
treats me too well.
(I can tell.)

"Cedric, don't count your tips in public."
~ Home Alone

* * *

I Count My Tips in Public

the one with a great vantage point sighed;
    she told me to rest
the one who looks with worried eyes held me;
    he said you are the best
the one who doesn't speak his mind looked me in the eye;
    he said be true
the one I see but once a year shook his head;
    he said be careful what you do
the one who looks like me left quick;
    she said it's all okay
the one whose will is strong just laughed;
    he said come back some day
the one who dances in the night returned;
    he said speak with gratitude
the one whose youth belies his age smiled;
    he said make love your food
the one who can't remember much called me;
    she said just read
the one who goes the distance listened;
    she said do what you need.

and so I listened carefully
I did what they were saying
though it's rude, I count my tips in public
because they didn't know they were paying.

Lost

flesh of my flesh
bone of my bone
I fight for your return
angry and alone
paper of blades
cuts at my heart
twisted and rank
and set in stone
a dark kind of blue
shadows my world
screams tear the night
on every step of the dark trail
to misery

In Honor of a September Wedding

In peace may your souls forever be.
As celestial bodies converge as one,
simply dance; in beauty move.
For no greater joy do we behold
than in a bright and simple ring of gold
that humbly, but surely stands to prove
in time, one and one
can yield
infinity.

photo by the author

Cecile J. Quasar is a graphic designer and artist. She admits to writing poetry often but rarely reading poems, preferring sci-fi, humor and fantasy novels as well as non-fiction articles. The poetry in this book was collected from 17 years' worth of writings and illustrated with drawings by the author. Ms. Quasar received a B.F.A. in graphic design at University of Missouri–St. Louis. She lives in St. Louis, Missouri with her family. This is her first book.

The author's web site:
www.thewigglytree.com

Send email to the author:
wigglytree@gmail.com

This book was set in Cochin. The fonts used on the cover are Cochin, Garamond Premier Pro and Angelic Serif. The book's layout was done in Adobe InDesign. The illustrations were drawn with fine-point gel pens and edited in Adobe Photoshop. The cover art was drawn in pencil, painted with Grambacher watercolors, and embellished with Prismacolor pencils. The author designed the book and its cover and painted the cover art.

www.ingramcontent.com/pod-product-compliance
Lightning Source LLC
Chambersburg PA
CBHW061724020426
42331CB00006B/1078